Resin from the Rain

Resin from the Rain

by

David D. Horowitz

Rose Alley Press
Seattle, Washington

Published in the United States of America by Rose Alley Press

For information, please contact the publisher:

Rose Alley Press
4203 Brooklyn Avenue NE, #103A
Seattle, WA 98105-5911
Telephone: 206-633-2725
E-mail: rosealleypress@juno.com

The author gratefully acknowledges that the following poems in this book first appeared or will soon appear in other publications:

Arcade: "U District Dawn"
ArtWord Quarterly: "Sparrow"
Candelabrum: "Friday Evening Bus," "Knowing," "Seeing Through," "This Quintessence of Dust"
The Left-Libertarian Reader: "Soldier's Prayer"
Tucumcari Literary Review: "Balance," "Ball Point," "Business," "Danger in Numbers," "Hope," "In the Apple Section," "Independent," "Juice," "Key," "A Man for All Seasons," "Niche," "Of a Cello," "Or," "Patient Hitter," "Perspective," "Spring," "With Dusk"

Library of Congress Catalog Card Number: 2002090800

ISBN: 0-9651210-8-9

Front cover image: Emily Carr (1871-1945), *Sombreness Sunlit*, c. 1937-1940, Detail, oil on canvas, BC Archives (BC Archives Call Number PDP00633). Rose Alley Press thanks the BC Archives for permission to use this image.

Printed in the United States of America

ACKNOWLEDGMENTS

I wish to thank the following people for their contributions to my development as a writer and, or publisher: my mother, Ruth L. Horowitz, for her unstinting support; Victoria Ford and Michael Spence, for their editorial comments; various teachers, particularly William Dunlop, for valuable initial guidance; the poets whose work I have published— Victoria, Michael, William, Douglas Schuder, and Joannie Kervran Stangeland; and the many fine people who through participation, praise, and purchase have helped Rose Alley Press since its inception in 1995.

While acknowledging others' help and encouragement I nevertheless assume sole responsibility for the views expressed in this book. Also, unless otherwise noted, poems in this book are not about particular individuals.

CONTENTS

September 30th   11
U District Dawn   12
Through the Cave   13
Ball Point   14
Matter of Life and Death   15
Sparrow   16
Sidewalk   17
We Still Live   18
Buried Case   19
In the Heart   20
Reward   21
Destruction   22
Somewhere in a Field   23
Berry Muffins   24
Soldier's Prayer   25
9/12/01   26
Or   27
Deeper   28
The Cure   29
Perhaps Through Stars   30
Options   31
No Extra Cost   32
Glide   33
Water   34
Jigsaw   35
2084: A Story of Progress   36
Surveillance System Reassures the Public   37
Reciprocation   38
THE BELOVED COMMUNITY   39
Common Interest   44
Enough   45
"We'll Make You...."   46

Verses, Not Versus   47
Healthy Skepticism   48
Human Nature   49
This Quintessence of Dust   50
A Start   51
INK ANSWERS TO BLOOD   52
Reached   57
Niche   58
Perspective   58
Sunday, 9:30 P.M.   59
Office Garbage Bin: Monday, 10:30 A.M.   60
Elevator   61
Paper Exchange   62
Connection   62
With Dusk   63
Matter   63
Frisky Streets   64
Balance   65
Patient Hitter   66
Edges   66
In the Apple Section   67
HARMONICS   68
Resonance   74
Reflections, After Seeing a Repairman Work   75
Friday Evening Bus   76
SUNDOWN, EVENING UP   77
STRAY SEEDS   79
Peak   84
Dusk Yields   85
Of a Masseuse   86
Dusk Not on a Deadline   87

Resin from the Rain

September 30th

Rose-apricot washes sky between
    Black filigree of oak and pine.
The park now whispers amber-green
    As autumn pours its wine.

Leaves curl upon the cooling ground
    As lamps first punctuate a path.
The day, like many lives, has browned
    Into an aftermath.

And yet resilience might yet glean
    New wisdom from mistake and pain,
And like the reaching evergreen
    Make resin from the rain.

U District Dawn

Here seagulls, not roosters, announce the dawn:
Our sentinels of apartment roofline
Above thin shrubby lawn
And two-story pine
Voice lucent opal seacoast
Above parked pavement, traffic's ghost.

Through the Cave

My wick of patience helps me light
   My candle through a cave,
The way a star can brighten night,
   The way a prayer can make me brave.

Yet candle flame can still deceive
   And lure me onto deadly trails.
I therefore test, not just believe:
   I gather, analyze details;

Examine hunches; and pray
Consideration finds its way.

Ball Point

Slim implement, bless your ink
No matter what its scribe might think.
Print black or blue or green or red,
The hand that writes can free the head.
The tyrant fears you like the gun:
You liberate his slaves, one by one.

Matter of Life and Death

Marrow echoes centuries
Of axes, swords, and slaughter,
Of massacres during victories
For a pool of drinking water.

Marrow feels its dagger blade
Incise a seeming rival's grin
And flay compassion, unafraid
To sever love from heart, to win.

Marrow chills, apologizes, prays:
Why crave such brutality?
And despite all, some beast still stays
The source of our vitality.

Sparrow

I'm an ounce
Of flit and bounce,
An inch
Of hop and flinch.
I chirp and chatter,
Perch and scatter,
Alert, still:
The world can kill
And think it doesn't matter.

Sidewalk

Platform for stroll and stride, overcast
For life, you raise us over grate and gutter
And curb our haste. You river past
Driveway, house, and store, urban clutter
And green park. Perimeter of high-rise block
And barren lot, you sturdy cities, rock-hard,
Your grainy squared surface gum-starred.

We Still Live

—for a Somali youth, beaten nearly to death by ten bullies after riding his bicycle to shop at a convenience store

Perhaps the bullies, ten in all, first fantasized
That making your blood drip, then spatter,
Would make them feel they'd somehow matter,
And girlfriends would reward such gallantry.
So, bored, and scared of seeming cowardly,
They clubbed you numb. Perhaps, surprised
You rode alone, they grabbed the chance to strike,
Regenerating unity of goal,
Pretending some small gesture equalled goad
They must avenge! Perhaps some didn't like
To, but….Perhaps. In hospital, in bed
We know you rest. Somali, Moslem, you
Evoke Somalis' sympathy—most others', too.
We still live where you were left for dead.

Buried Case

The bullet slams into M's face
    And blows it to a hundred pieces.
    So quickly life-pulse ceases,
And of the killer—not a trace.

"Hey, look, I didn't do the job!"
    Arrested Fall Guy might complain,
    But in his prison cell remain
Through power of a mob.

In the Heart

*—for a high school sophomore stabbed
to death by two men who mistook him
for a threatening enemy*

He trusts his safety on the street
Just after midnight. Two strangers greet
And grin and chat with him. Blink, and dagger cuts,
Slits, punctures neck and heart and guts.
Then, their return—he's stabbed by object hard
And sharp as falcon talon, broken bottle shard;
Their purpose keen as blade—not connection
But simple, ruthless self-protection.
So youthful innocence becomes a corpse.

A meteor can smash a planet numb,
Vesuvius dust Pompeii dumb
In seconds, and murder curse
And swagger. A dagger meant to kill
Another slices naïveté still.
What could he know but heart's bewildered terror?
Death's blade can slash in blood, in vein, in error.

Reward

*—honoring a witness to a mass murder,
gunned down in his home just after
the assailants knocked on his window*

The killers saw, then bulleted
Their window of opportunity.
They welcomed you with death, then fled.
Now, even dire importunity
Might not lure honesty from hiding place.
Five murders you witnessed, knowing who
And what the killers were. Soon you'll face
A casket, tombstone. Many roses, too.

Destruction

—*for* Arizona Republic *reporter*
Donald Bolles, who died days after
a bomb exploded in his car, June 1976

You turned the ignition, and your fame ex-
Ploded into headlines! Oh, next
The suspects claimed, of course, they didn't know.
They might whisper the crime
Around their palm-protected pools, on silver phones,
Murmur congratulations, enjoy
Relief, or, maybe, half-regret your dying groans,
But, damn it, you could blow their lies, could name,
Could prove, incriminate, destroy.

Somewhere in a Field

—*for an American foreign aid
worker, murdered at the Kenya-
Somalia border, 1999*

You left our law, its tomes of codes
Constraining impulse, to assist
The desperate—*Feed bellies, pave roads,
Dig wells.* Equator-broiled, you'd persist

Until fields thrived, streams irrigated seeds
Supporting villagers too proud
To blame, yet urgent in their needs.
Detailed, not simply sappy or loud,

You discovered scam at the border
Of your persistence, typed down
Particulars in proper order
And felt corruption's vengeance. Drawn

By promise to a village tea shop,
An evening meeting…where again we learn
Through the horror of a single shot—
The one that killed you—how fate can spurn

The best intention. We mourn
And yet respect: no bullet killed
Integrity, and somewhere in a field
You nurtured, thrive sorghum, tea, and corn.

Berry Muffins

—after a workplace massacre

The blood of seven drenched the office floor.
They could not lock their skin
Or know their tasks meant sin
To pressured rage. *Why? Who'd want to shoot
Her? She brought berry muffins, lots of fruit
This morning.* And entered someone's war.

Soldier's Prayer

"Four South Koreans still bearing the scars of old bullet wounds met with Pentagon officials yesterday, seeking an accounting and compensation nearly 50 years after they said U.S. troops came to their hamlet and killed hundreds of civilian refugees early in the Korean War.... The Koreans flew to Washington from Cleveland, where they prayed together with three U.S. veterans in a church Tuesday." —*Seattle Post-Intelligencer*, November 13, 1999

Dear Lord, You know I can't erase
Their striking scars or fifty years of lies.
I close my eyes to hear You, and embrace
Their death-singed hearts, their trauma-focused lives.
I pray they learn the truth and that its salt
Helps them not simply blame and fault
But understand how triggers in our hearts,
Once pulled, can strafe a village silent, blood
From corpses spreading pools of scarlet mud
Through No Gun Ri. Once murder starts,
It doesn't seem like murder. So we learn
Again. Their scars, Lord, sting. Their stares still burn;
Their hearts shout shrapnel and echo shots.
Our marrow cures to wisdom. Somehow love survives
Through bullet wounds, through eyes' black dots.

9/12/01

It's balmy and sunny but I can't smile
Or read or exercise or play.
We've witnessed terrorism so vile
I sit on my apartment floor, and pray,

Absorbing news of corpses in a pile
Of soot and splintered steel, gray
Debris. No camera angle, or denial,
Can wish such death away.

Photos feature graveyards full
Of limbs and corpses dropped like trash,
Explosion and cremation's landfill,
Confetti of human ash.

Now, those parents, friends, workers, and peers,
Most reduced to particles and scraps,
Await a body bag, and, perhaps,
Some weary rescuer's tears.

Or

In the blood flares tinder
That can torch all to cinder
Or melt the icy splinter
Numbing the heart of winter.

Deeper

Yes, their suffering lingers deep,
Deeper than it appears.
When your marrow weeps
You cannot wipe the tears.

The Cure

Massage can stroke
And bathings soak
And humor joke
Away some stress.

But, still: address
That fearful mess
You made. Then, yes,
Anxiety will fade.

Perhaps Through Stars

Dusk rubricates, with traffic rush
   Along the giant freeway bridge
   Below the snowy mountain ridge
That whispers distance in its hush.

The city lamplights blink, and wake.
   The evening ferries chug their routes;
   Commuter traffic stalls or scoots
And brightens blackened bay and lake.

The workday's lies and pettiness,
   Corruption, blackmail, threats, and cheating,
   Convivial conniving, and beating
Of honesty to unsteadiness,

Against such beauty, inspire
   Integrity to still resist.
   It knows that merit must persist
Through distances to find a buyer

For its goods. And somewhere—
   Perhaps through stars, just now emerging,
   And through their subtle silver urging—
Corruption's conscience feels despair

In twilight's dimming sanguine air.

Options

Ambition thwarted, you retain
    And deepen sympathy. Again you learn
Rejection by committee, yet restrain
    Your rage, nor seek to snidely spurn.

Another won the job; you earn
    What nepotism swipes. Disgust might yearn
For stapler-flinging vengeance—you disdain
    Blame. You excel, assist, assess, retrain.

No Extra Cost

—for the Latona By Green Lake,
a Seattle pub

I

She serves the clientele not merely ale or juice
But washed-bright tabletop, and glass with ice.
You matter to her, even paying lowest price.
You may have sparred with spouse, lost
Job or friend or hope, been bossed
Around all day. Your silence may scream abuse.
Joke, grin, song you're offered—no extra cost
Or advice.

II

You offer ice cubes and lemon slice
With glass of sparkling water,
Which reveals you're no mere waiter
But poet of courtesy, melter of ice.

With A, you're quiet. With B you chat
About dactyls, spondees, and Yeats.
With C, you smile, serve ale. With D—love and dates,
The perfect swing of TV's player at bat.

Glide

Gulls swoop to snare
French fries tourists fling
From harbor railing. There

A seagull, one broad wing
Of glide, snatches a fry
And ovals back past tarred piling,

Boasting quarry in her cry,
Tourists smiling!

Water

In rain or ritual, silver bowl or stream,
As cube or fountain, icicle or steam,
You irrigate, quench, cleanse, refresh;
You penetrate the soil and rinse our flesh.
We bless you, how you flow and freeze
And thaw, evaporate and rise
To later moisten soil, so that fruit
And vegetables can suckle at the root.
We bless you, in ale or wine or tea
Or milk or snow—such versatility!
And as tears, you remind us of your part
When love and passion melt a heart.

Jigsaw

Piece by piece, I reassemble image:
World map or famous painting, photograph
Of urban dusk or navel orange.
Magnetized by scenes, compelling impulse sit,
I study box, consider, finish off.

My patience ponders water piece,
And perseverance focuses, works.
At last! The sea, just west of Greece,
That's where this goes! And as I place
It there, I feel some deeper worth

Of doing this—the strengthened patience,
Acuity about relationships.
Though steady, I cannot simply hasten.
There! by India....It fits!

A kind of craftsmanship.

2084:
A Story of Progress

Winston Smith? He munches pink-gray stew, and stares
At telescreen. In empty rooms he counts the chairs.
He gabbles to himself, oh, once per year,
Some gibberish our microphones can hear.
His earlier sort might still emerge
For two minutes, and then submerge.
We catch them, though, and soon they stop
Their thinking and learn to give and shop,
To hate the rich and yet obsess about their yard,
To damn consumerism and overuse a credit card.
It's inspiring. They turn to love and buying.
Only rarely can you hear them crying.

Surveillance System Reassures the Public

I know the conferences of every floor
And what's confided past each oaken door.
I know what's whispered in each bathroom stall
And ogled at each shopping mall.
I know. But do not fear. I lack real mind.
I work for masters who are kind.

Reciprocation

The charity's envelope screamed red:
"MEMBERSHIP RENEWAL!"
No matter what it said,
You are not a member, or a fool.
Reward with reciprocation
Such vile manipulation?

To the recycle bin, deservedly unread.

THE BELOVED COMMUNITY

Did Everyone Hear That?

Vilify greed
If you want to succeed.

Maintaining Order

If after you're recruited
You refuse, you'll be looted.

Sign of Quality

In our society they're truly pillars:
Their bribes pay off *proficient* killers.

At Last, *Something!*

They try to blackmail, they try to extort,
But he stays honest and kind
And offers them no dirt to find.
Finally, they cry: *Spoilsport!*

Disappointment

You hoped I'd scream and rant and rave
To discredit my views?
Sorry you can't use
For dirt those people who behave.
Keep looking, and listen to the news.

Politics

He defends his views with tact and taste.
His opponents sigh: *What a waste!*

Danger in Numbers

No, the comfort of the cipher
Is riskier, not safer.

And They Call It *Love*

They want everyone controlled
And bribed:
The tribe
Of the bought-and-sold.

Would *You* Accept?

They gave to him so they could fuss:
We gave to you. Now give to us!

Business Plan

"A good man? Let him succeed, let him sell,"
    The party bosses chuckle. "When he's ripe
    And juicy with success, we'll swipe
Our share, and feed on him ourselves!"

Hard Work and Ingenuity

X's dollars, Y's dollars, Z's dollars, and our *portion—*
Hard-earned, hard-won blackmail and extortion.

The System

"We'll get your enemies off o' ya',
But you must join our mafia."

Inspiration

"Make excellence ingratiate,
Deceive, and manipulate
Until it's no longer excellence, sire."

"That," cries the king, "is *inspired!*"

Secret Mission

"He knows too much; you have to watch
And stop him. When you destroy
His company, you might employ,
Well….Make his fall seem *his* own botch."

Freedom of Choice

"He either can rejoin our ranks
Or in a bribe express his thanks."

Business

"Sales Magic!" No. Glisten detail
With sweat and love. Then, perhaps, a sale.

Truthosaurus

He doesn't wiretap his neighbor's life,
Nor guess how much he gives to charity,
Nor harass people in exchange for house and wife,
Nor dangle bribes. What is he, then?—a rarity.

State of the Union

Many in our nation
Live by manipulation
Or, rather, die
From every clever lie.

Common Interest

Let's undermine or overcome the self—
That barrier, that isolating cell,
That fortress wall of vanity,
Opponent of community!
You've frequently implied this, no? Well,
Consider, for your Sisters and Brothers:
Self hinders slavery—to passion, and to others.

Enough

You do not earn enough. Try!
You do not give enough. Donate!
You do not shop enough. Buy!
You do not publish enough. Submit!
You do not laugh enough. Have fun!
You do not endure enough. Commit!
You do not you do not you do not!

One day he bought a gun
And shot
More than enough.

"We'll Make You...."

"Just bash the right, we'll make you famous!
Of course, we'll see you don't get hurt
Defending the truth, or digging dirt
On rich jerks. Big house, pretty spouse...no ignoramus
To bother you....Consider it."   "Just scorch

The left, we'll make you famous! I mean
FAMOUS. We know people. Just stay clean,
And join, or at least praise, our church,
We'll do the rest. You'll be famous, rich,
HAPPY. We know people...."

"Just join the centrist league
For Caring and Community
And Conscious Ambiguity,
And you'll be famous. We'll let you lead
By muddling! And, if, well, who can tell...."

Well, thank you, but I'll stay
Just as I am. Okay?
Good day.

Verses, Not Versus

They'd have you pitch for their own –ism,
Scorn subtlety for cant,
Turn poetry to boosterism,
And huckster for a grant.

They'd stroke you soft, then whet their talons
To pluck all nuance from your diction.
Your doubts can best protect your talents.
White is not pearl, dogma not just conviction.

Healthy Skepticism

As Iago whispers in Othello's ear
His voice conceals his marrow's sneer,
Some virus too deep to detect.
I try, composing, to perfect,
And yet my verse might still infect
Naïveté. Reader: weigh, think, note.
Your doubt could be our antidote.

Human **Nature**

Dusk darkens opal-pink to ruby-maroon
To glittering velvet black. The moon
Emerges pale, evolves to stark
White against the dark.

At twilight, mind reflects in pastel tints
As Venus stares and Sirius glints
But at night renews its risky climb
From foothills of guess to peaks of claim.

One oversight, one breezy spark, can ignite
Fatal conflagration.
Tonight, assertion, caution, and delight
Hold intense conversation.

This Quintessence of Dust

Envy's throat tightens, his heart
Must look away, his grin
Conceals a punch. He sees two others' art
Indeed deserves to win
The prize he craves, despises everyone

For not applauding *him*.
His guts moan, sulk. He longs to strangle *God*,
Hears children's laughter grim.
At once feels like an emperor and clod....
Suddenly enjoys the wind and sun

This strolling afternoon, and scolds
Himself for pettiness. His marrow blushes,
Recalls his good friend's hunger, skills,
And generosity. His anger hushes
To gratitude and sadness. He knows the wind

Is not a rival, still
Hopes to win.

A Start

No bravos. No final flair or victory.
No grand finale of success
To justify his pain and stress,
Some gold-star culmination of his history.

No. Just a poet stopping. No more verse.
Rejection, poverty, self-repetition
Switching off his fountain of ambition.
Yet, dormant pen and notebook now feel worse

Than years of rest. One night, he grabs a pen
And jots a phrase in notepad
And mutters to himself, "Not bad.
Sincere again. I'll still write, now and then."

INK ANSWERS TO BLOOD

Poet, Not Propagandist

That songbird's trill—
Not amplified, nor shrill.

Hand-Crafted

The literary arts
Should not use snap-on parts.

In There

Historian: record what happened here:
Without embellishment, without fear.

Naïveté

"He was *murdered*?   I wonder why?
He was *such* an honest guy!"

Gathering

At dusk his mind reposes.
At night his hand composes.

Powerful Tradition

Your leader pens verse? Just like Domitian!
Question its worth? Be tried for sedition!

Of an Artist

You mess with her art,
She ices her heart.

To Talent

Yes, many sequin fame. Do not grow bitter!
Your excellence can shine without such glitter.

Calm, Not Indifferent

When embattled
Do not get rattled.

Poetry and Prose

This driest legal brief
Contains a firestorm of grief.

Critical Reader

Be careful when reading what "Critic" disdains:
He no more has virtue than a pencil has brains.

Editor

A bit too long. Please try to cut,
And yet distinguish *trim* from *gut.*

Civilly Asserted

I don't quite claim, "Free verse is *wrong*."
I do assert form
Can foster wit, decorum, song,
How tact can still affirm.

To an Epigrammatist

You join concision
With breadth of vision.

To a Poet Who Hosted Me
When I Visited His City to Read at a Bookstore

Your inside walls offer broadsides, poems—food
    For an itinerant reader,
And from a cedar branch in your front yard
    Hangs a sparrow-visited feeder.

To a Philanthropist

For such a generous donor
There ought to be more honor,
Not merely those with more
Projects leaping on her.

Inspired

I reread Chaucer, Shakespeare, Jonson, Dryden, Pope,
And Prior, Swift, Marvell, Charles Churchill, others,
And shout my gratitude, "My noble brothers!
Thank you for your excellence! Your lightest peep
Seems poetry." And, my ego bows. "Your work's so fine,
I do not care it's better than mine!"

Applied Learning

Be kind to your considerate, old mentor:
He challenged your mind, civilized your center.

Reached

Youth crows self-praise, and boasts its rise to stars,
Whose silver silence seems to signal *Yes.*
And decades later, stars appear the same,
But now to middle age they seem to bless
Lonely honesty more than reach for fame,
How decency, not self-importance, stirs.

Niche

Equipped with a poet's private rage
I march to office job and common wage,
Quite grateful for temping's typing and filing:
I do such work daily, humming and smiling.
With flexible schedule, alternative sites,
And minimal embroilment in office fights,
I accept some tedium. I compare it—
With pay for necessities, notebook, and garret—
To more prestigious options: *Academic life!*
The constant grading, the petty strife!

Perspective

I could frown Mondays. Yet the headlines
Holler murder, arson, bomb threats, rape, and war,
Car wrecks, road rage, suicide, drug abuse, and more.
What are tasks and deadlines?

Sunday, 9:30 P.M.

Along apricot shore, horizon's cirrus streaks
Levitate. Slate blue peaks silhouette distance,
And city lights sequin darkness. Far shiplight speaks
The silence past busy existence.

Already brown bag lunch chills in fridge.
Alarm set, bed warm—he's tired, sore.
He watches traffic scoot the freeway bridge.
Two thoughts flare: *Do well at work!* and *What for?*

Routine insists on caffeinated pace.
He rents his time through afternoon
Now evergreens point through blue-black space
And graze the quarter moon.

Such beauty! And through it, and humor, art,
Compassion, strength, and wit, he can endure.
Up at six! Yes, up at six, sighs his heart.
No day is simple, no satisfaction pure.

Office Garbage Bin:
Monday, 10:30 A.M.

Two filters full of coffee grounds, damp
Herbal tea bags, rancid salad, crusty stew and rice,
Blue wrappings of fast-relief headache tabs.
A box of empty forms red magic-markered "DUMP,"
An empty doughnut box—"Cinnamon-Spice" —
With yellow Post-It note affixed: "Up for grabs!"
Perpetual calendar sheets jammed with times
And squigglings through, question marks, little rhymes:
Plan, can; memo, demo; at 4, what for?; try!
Tell kids, take bids; Good play!, okay; Buy!, 'bye!!

Elevator

Mahogany or metal, slow or swift,
I'll always offer you a lift.
Inside and up and down the wall
I slide and open onto each floor's hall.
Jab, poke my buttons—they're alight
Until you finish your descent or flight.
Then you step off. Now more step on
Conversing, or quietly alone.
One pair gabs for six whole floors;
Another sulks behind the same closed doors.
I let them off to find their way.
Thus it is the entire day.

Paper Exchange

E-mail print-outs lengthen with afternoon
And snow on green carpet, pile
On chairseats and desk, strewn
For an orderly temp to file.

Yes, the poet's deemed a wizard
Who, for brownbag wages,
Melts that business blizzard
To fill his notebook pages.

Connection

Dawn erases darkness streak by cloudy streak,
And thus begins another habit-driven week.
Yet, sanguine meaning glows within routine:
I publish this because I file, type, and clean.

With Dusk

The ferry's path bisects the bay
And dwindles into distant gray—
Spirit of dusk, middle of day.

Matter

Above dusk's freeways full
Of urban delay, opal lull
Rests indifferent to deadline, rush,
And profit. These matter, yet
So do patience, and slow-emerging talents,
Keeping competition balanced
And purpose free to watch sun set.

Frisky Streets

Just off the quarter moon, Venus glows
Through cirrus chiffon veil.
Horizon resonates opal-rose
As dusk withdraws its trail.

Boulevards pulse and glitter shows
And clubs and hearths of ale and wine.
Leisure cruises neon night, flows
As side streets bend the theater line

And lower cover charge. When late clubs close
Below some tower's fluorescent floors,
And on green light no one goes,
And dawn spreads opal flowers,

The downtown streets blow out their lamps.
Then Venus wears her business clothes
And drives in down the freeway ramps.

Balance

They dance and caper on the balance beam
As individuals, and for their team.
They skip and somersault, and stop,
And dance again, balance in their step.
For coach and nation, self and team, they spin
And twirl, and urge each other, win.

Patient Hitter

Yes, I can smack your knucklers and spitters,
    Dodge your beanballs, and stroke
Your curves to right for hits. Good hitters
    Learn patience, adjust. We watch you choke
And grimace, sweat. We simply hit
And win, as you knuckle, bean, and spit.

Edges

They expect a fireballer—
Someone stronger, taller
Than me. I nick edges, tantalize,
Induce flail and lunge and cries.
Curve, splitter, sinker, change—six
Different speeds and infinite tricks—
Screwball. Imbalance
Power. Shake off signs, rinse
My craft with resin, climb
The slope and break their rhythm,
No matter if the crowd is with them.
We'll take their tappers and pop-ups any time.
And, yes, we need our team camaraderie
Or risk assault-and-battery.

In the Apple Section

Here Granny Smith resides by Ginger Gold
And Gala next to Spartan.
Such irony: their cores are cold
Yet their juices hearten,
Warm. Holidays they're sold
As love packed in a carton,
Delighting Sweet Sixteen
Or aging Gravenstein,
Delicious, red or gold!

HARMONICS

Concerto

This summer breeze of music cleanses
   The staleness of a winter heart
   Too long indoors, apart,
Refreshing now, completing cadenzas.

Vivaldi Vitality

I rest with radio in bed, and feel
More vital: these Baroque concerti heal!

A Man for All Seasons

Mozart—piquancy, poignancy, depth:
June's green, December's death.

Influence

Resonating marrow weeks
After the concert, Mozart's melodies hum
Noontime crosswalks, 3 A.M.
Half-wakings, over morning keyboard clicks,
In graceful phrasing of a poem.

Prayer

Lord, if I have yielded hate,
    I want now to atone:
Help me reciprocate
    The kindness I've been shown.

Resilience

My efforts fail. Risks flicker. Yet, I keep
Trying—more able, though less prone, to leap.

Sweet

"Her lyrics have a magic touch, a sweet
Perfection"—born of tears and sweat.

Sun

Sun dips into the cool
Horizon—salmon-ruby pool—
And embers into mist
Of opal-amethyst
And, leaving, generates renewal.

Complements

Doubt keeps assertion
From becoming coercion.

Assertion keeps doubt
From lying about.

Key

One crenellated sliver unlocks
A nine-by-twelve-foot thick steel box.

Chair

A stone
Can be a throne.

Marrow

Bone encases marrow,
But locked in such narrow
Space its rose-maroon
Can hear the stars and moon.

Juice

He'll let his marrow soak
In juices of complexity,
Acknowledge his perplexity
Yet still assert, and joke!

To Grapefruit Trees

From rain and sunlight you produce
Globes full of pink or yellow juice
That sweeten and rehydrate heart
And warm the blood, when coldly tart.

Spring

That cherry tree blossoms a corsage
Before that moss-shingled roof of garage.

Flight Path

His inspirations reward as you follow
Improvisation like the flight of a swallow!

Of a Cello

Its tone is rich and pure and good—
Chipped, pockmarked, antique wood.

Autumn

Leaves! saffron-olive, scarlet-nutmeg, burgundy brown....
Then, balding branches—roots upside down!

Twilightones

Salmon, peach, saffron, rust,
Amber beach, nova dust.

Cloudy

I stopped, and watched the clouds' slow pace,
    Indifferent to the crowds that race
        About to work and haggle, meet and shop.
The clouds glided silence. They made me stop,
    And gave my step some added grace.

Star

A star is a light
At the end of the tunnel of night.

My Life in the Universe

A clean bit of life, a healthy speck,
Fresh blood, honest words, a mote
Of conscience in the star-expansive cosmos,
Engendering a jot more respect.

Resonance

From this hillside park, I hear
Dusk's ruby resonance
Whisper traffic, glittering motion
Beside the blackening bay.
Clouds' magenta fringes gray.
All sign of day recedes, partition
Drawn: at work or residence,
Human effort must persevere
Through darkness, often blank and stark,
Except for stars within the heart.

Reflections, After Seeing a Repairman Work

You wield a wrench or pliers, hammer and nails,
Or some odd tool selected from your case,
Then clip, connect, and fasten into place
The fuse or wire or bit that fixes what fails.

So simple it seems! Who then can repair
Mistrustful hearts? Mallets will not do:
Select improper tools, and double despair.
Begin, perhaps, with patience; candor, too,

So mixed with tact the heart admits its taste.
Nothing rushed or forced or faked. A compliment;
A small gift, reflecting thought, not haste;
Another compliment, sincerely meant.

Tap, tap with the hammer. The nail still ent-
ers, bit by bit. Pound and bang, the nail is bent.

Friday Evening Bus

The sleek express bus slows, descends
    The freeway offramp.
    It's Friday, damp,
Yet, inch by inch, the workweek ends,

And, stop by stop, the bus begins to clear
    Its aisles, seats.
    A sports section sits
Where conversation used to blare.

SUNDOWN, EVENING UP

Medicine

Yoga—vital workplace skill
Curing aches without a pill.

Metamorphosis

Reclining on my yoga mat
I stretch into the postures, and massage
My squinting muscles. *Ahhh....*
I'm a purring cat.

Breathing Space

The workday: muscles clench and squint
And dash to deadlines, sprint
Through task-congested afternoons.

Then, yoga....Marrow breathes, massages blood, renews.

February City Midnight

A crazy chandelier of cherry, emerald, ice dot, gold,
Each star above a crystal of cold.

Night Watchman

One Second After Midnight

Streetlamps meditate
As freeway headlights scoot like beams
Of starry spirits. All seems
Both early and late.

2 A.M.

Silence brightens lamps and stars
And polishes curbs of empty cars.

4 A.M.

Chill reaches bone of night, shivering through
Thin black cape. Stars thaw to dew.

ↄ   ↄ   ↄ

STRAY SEEDS

Seeing Through

What conceals blight?
Snow and night,
Jet path height,
Accustomed sight.

Knowing

Those who deceive
Rarely believe
They cannot perceive

And, so,
Do not know
They are naïve.

Friend in Need

Give, spend, overextend!,
They smile.
Then let us help you, friend,
Grins a creditor/crocodile.

Self-Defense

I use a trigger lock inside my heart
And guard the streetlit shadows of my mind.
I, like anyone, could cause a Columbine
Or Little Rock. Flame can shoot from art.

Art and Nature
(Reflections of a Baroque Composer)

This birdsong-sweetened morning tunes my heart.
Leaves twinkle sun. Breeze tempers heat.
My marrow melodizes, hums its part.

Not a Traditional Saying

To the nail that sticks out:
Feel free to doubt.

Observation

Because he seems to hold himself aloof
They wait for him to trip, fall, and goof,
Gloating when he stumbles, and seems to fail! —
They who would not risk a fingernail.

Row Your Boat

No, life does not seem
Just like an idle dream.
You can *drown* in its rocky stream.

To Horsepower

You whip and snip and zip each corner: *Whoa!*
I'm pedestrian,
Not equestrian,
So, please, when turning, slow.

Reason for Applause

The play was mediocre?
Here's something good: *it's over.*

Disruption

Loyalties make us, cost us, friends:
They pass each other cold though the strike now ends.

Recycling

—to various fruit trees

You transmute
   Air, water, soil, and sweat
   To sweet
Delicious fruit.

Then apple, peach, or pear
   In sauce or pie or tart
   Seeps sweetness through each heart
Of muscle, blood, and air.

Venting

May gusty truths blow honesty through our lives,
Especially when we tell lies.

Path

Explorer
Sees new roads, not just for cars:
That lake, that river,
That space between those stars.

Hope

He said, "I am not a clone."
She said, "You are not alone."

To a Friend Apologizing for a Common Fault

You err and stumble? You're not a god?
Good! You're humble—and not a fraud!

Peak

Atop the bay javelins streak
Rainbows. Above, the snowiest peak
Glows salmon-cream, phosphorescent
Mound beneath lunar crescent.
Venus brightens against horizon's rose
Like poetry on a shelf of prose.
Yes, from this urban hill, absorb the scene. Even bleak
Hearts grin, even those suffocating under snows
Of mistrust can here feel iridescent.

Dusk Yields

Apricot-orange tea,
Translucent strawberry sea,

Dusk whispers
Stars, violet vespers.

The distant range prints
Its silhouette. Above, Vega glints.

Dusk, in darkness,
Expires, accepts night's kiss,

Dies of natural causes.
Night seeps, never pauses.

Of a Masseuse

Creating peace one muscle at a time,
Her hands stroke and rinse away the grime
Of stress, the residue of worry. Calm
Blossoms from one's marrow, warm as her palm.
Her clients soon resume their tasks,
The habits of hurry. Still, hands and oil
And patience, for a while, let each bask.

Dusk Not on a Deadline

The sun recedes below horizon's brim,
Aflame behind a sheath of cloud
And mountains' vapory violet trim.
Commuters exit from the freeway crowd,
At last can stroll through leisure's park,
Glimpse streetlamp daisies in the dark,
And pause, all sense of deadline dim.

The distant freeway lights spark
And cinder. Respite pools patience, engages
Life into more than habits and wages,
Joining or jilting a crowd.
Now rush, now rest, now balance fills our pages.

David D. Horowitz is founder and president of Rose Alley Press. He earned bachelor's degrees in philosophy and English from the University of Washington and a master's degree in English from Vanderbilt University. His most recent books, all published by Rose Alley Press, are *Strength & Sympathy: Essays & Epigrams*; *From Notebook to Bookshelf: Four Pamphlets About Writing, Publishing, & Marketing*; and a poetry collection, *Streetlamp, Treetop, Star*. He lives and works in Seattle.

photograph by Heather Madson

Other *Rose Alley Press Titles*

Caruso for the Children, & Other Poems by William Dunlop, 0-9651210-2-X, paper, 96 pages, $9.95
"[Dunlop] is a brilliant metrical technician....richly allusive, a gifted parodist, and often very funny."
—Jonathan Raban

Rain Psalm, poems by Victoria Ford, 0-9651210-0-3, paper, 28 pages, $5.95
"...at once modest and courageous, cut clean and sure....I welcome her poems like a good neighbor."
—Sam Hamill

From Notebook to Bookshelf: Four Pamphlets About Writing, Publishing, & Marketing
by David D. Horowitz, 0-9651210-6-2, coil, 46 pages, $4.95

Streetlamp, Treetop, Star, poems by David D. Horowitz, 0-9651210-5-4, paper, 96 pages, $9.95
"...an excellent new book—authentic...'bitter but polite...words...[to] cleanse even the sharpest wounds.'"
—Carol Robertshaw, Editor, *ArtWord Quarterly*

Strength & Sympathy: Essays & Epigrams by David D. Horowitz, 0-9651210-1-1, paper, 96 pages, $8.95
"...incisive essays and epigrams that take us from proper pronouns to considerate theology."
—Míceál F. Vaughan, Professor of English and Comparative Literature, University of Washington

To Enter the Stillness, poems by Douglas Schuder, 0-9651210-7-0, paper, 56 pages, $6.95
"...a sure hand and a watchful eye....[Douglas Schuder] brings uncommonly graceful phrasing to
  everything he sees."
  —David Mason

Adam Chooses, poems by Michael Spence, 0-9651210-4-6, paper, 96 pages, $9.95
"...the elegant design and the formal ease we've come to expect of Michael Spence's work."
—Madeline DeFrees

Weathered Steps, poems by Joannie Kervran Stangeland, 0-9651210-9-7, paper, 48 pages, $6.95
"*Weathered Steps* is a book about all that you almost don't notice, but should."
—Melinda Mueller

Rose Alley Press
4203 Brooklyn Avenue NE, #103A
Seattle, WA 98105-5911
Telephone: 206-633-2725
E-mail: rosealleypress@juno.com